# Getting Around in the City

by Alma Flor Ada

illustrated by Ilja Bereznicks

**Harcourt**

Orlando   Boston   Dallas   Chicago   San Diego

Visit *The Learning Site!*

**www.harcourtschool.com**

I live in the city. It is a big,
busy place.

2

There are so many ways to get
around in the city!

There are many, many cars in
the city. Cars follow each other
in long lines.

4

Each car is different from the others.
Each driver is different, too!

Big trucks carry things around the
city. Each truck carries something
different. Some trucks carry gasoline.
Other trucks carry cement.

Some trucks carry fruits and vegetables to the supermarket. Can you guess what's inside the other trucks?

Lots of buses go around the city.
They carry grandparents and mothers
with babies.

They carry people going to work.
They carry shoppers with baskets from
the Chinatown market.

You can see lots of taxis in the city.
Some are yellow and some are other
colors.

Taxis carry people who are in a
hurry. The people may be going to
the airport.

Bicycles are everywhere in the city!
Some people on bicycles carry
important packages.

12

Other people on bicycles are getting
some exercise. They all need to be very
careful on busy city streets.

Some people ride the cable cars in the city. They smile as they ride.

The cable cars go up steep hills and down again. Riding a cable car looks like fun!

There are so many ways to get
around in the city! My favorite way
is to walk with my mother. We like
to watch the busy city around us!